RAISING THE ENERGIES
of Mother Earth
TOWARDS AND AFTER ASCENSION 2012

Raising the Energies of Mother Earth
Towards and After Ascension 2012

The Highest Truth

Victoria Cochrane

Victoria Cochrane

Raising the Energies of Mother Earth Towards and After Ascension 2012: The Highest Truth.

Category: New Age Publications; Ascension; the Universe.

Author: Victoria Cochrane.

Tasmania, Australia

ABN: 58 759 564 318

Copyright © Victoria Cochrane.

First Printed Balboa Press 2013.

Reprinted 2016 Victoria Cochrane Publications

All rights reserved. This book may not be reproduced in whole or in part, stored or posted on the internet or transmitted in any form or by any means without the express permission of the author or publisher of this book.

Edited by Victoria Cochrane.

Cover/interior graphics designed by Renea Stubbs.

Printed and bound by Lightening Source, Australia.

Distributed by Ingram Spark.

Cochrane, Victoria, 1960 –

www.victoriacochrane.com

https://victoriacochrane44.com

http://messagesfromotherworlds.blogspot.com

Email: victoriacochrane44@gmail.com

ISBN: 978-1-4525-0862-7

For Kris, Tristan and Will
May your lives on Earth be filled
with love and laughter, and your
onward soul journeys blessed with
learning, healing and
enlightenment.

Acknowledgements

This book would not have happened without the unexpected visit from a Fourth Plane being, Sheva, who had decided she wanted to show me the secrets of the universe. I am truly thankful to her for coming to me and for the lessons I learnt about ego and integrity along the way.

I give blessings and thanks to Master Saint Aloysius for trusting me to channel this book. I thank him for his patience and his faith in me. I acknowledge the masters of the Great Cosmic Council who have seen fit to bring these important messages to the world through me at this time. They have been with me every step of my journey, and I feel blessed and loved every day.

I cannot go without thanking my spiritual teacher and mentor, Rose Crane, whose wisdom and guidance have allowed me to grow into a healer and teacher in my own right. I thank her for telling me the truth with love. I also acknowledge the support of Jullie, who has become a great support and mentor to me over the last two years. I also give blessings to my spiritual family—Renea, Donna, Andie, Janelle, Ruth, Janelle, Lynnese, Shirley, Margaret, Kay, and Kelli—for giving me the encouragement I needed to continue and for being there to listen.

I also give thanks and blessings for my wonderful husband, Richy, who has supported me on this journey with patience and love. He is my twin flame and the keeper of my heart. He is with me every step of the way, and I am forever grateful.

Finally I give thanks and blessings to Creator, who has been steadfastly there in my life even when I have doubted him or myself. He is truly amazing, and his love has been the reason this book has come into being.

Victoria Cochrane

Contents

Foreword xi
Preface xiii

Part One
The Highest Truth:
Master Saint Aloysius

The Creator of All That Is 3
The Sacredness of Life 5
Safe 7
Unspoken Truths 9
The Dawning of Ages 11
Illumination 13
Ascended Masters 15
Blessings 17
Lessons 19
Deliverance 21
Babylon 25
Deity 27

Part Two
Messages from the Masters

The Greater Good 31
Ascension 33
The Lightbody 35
The Christ Consciousness 37
Living in the Light 39
The Concept of Oneness 41
Religion 43
The Violet Flame 45

The Four Sacred Elements

Water 49
Crystals 51
Amethyst Crystals and the Violet Flame 53
Fire 55
Earth 57
Air 59
Exchanging Energy 61
Time 63

About the Author 65

Foreword

I feel extremely privileged that my dear friend Victoria asked me to write the foreword for her first book. I am immensely proud of her, and I am blessed that she is an integral part of my spiritual family.

I first met Victoria over two years ago when I had been feeling lost and disconnected from life and, knowing this, had been asking for help and guidance. I immediately felt totally comfortable and safe with her even though I had never heard of Theta Healing, but the warmth Victoria radiated made me feel nurtured, and I instinctively knew I could trust her. The Theta work I have done with her since then has catapulted my spiritual growth in a way that I hadn't experienced before. I am truly grateful for the day Victoria was put on my path.

Victoria is very passionate about assisting people to live in their own truth with love, which in turn helps Mother Earth. Have an open heart as you read this book, and allow the words to integrate within. It really is simple: love yourself, and it will bring you warmth that will then radiate out to others.

Victoria speaks the truth of Spirit with love.

Many blessings,
Jullie Shepherd

In memory of my dear friend Jullie Shepherd, (1951-2015). Now a bright star in the sky. I will never forget you. Victoria.

Preface

This book has been centuries in the making. There are people who would wish that this information would remain unspoken, but the masters of the etheric realms, in consultation with our Creator, have deemed it time to reveal these truths that man has chosen to ignore.

The messages in this book are not my words. I have brought them through from Master Saint Aloysius and the masters of the Cosmic Council, who tell me that my agreement to write this book goes back beyond this lifetime. I have absolute faith and trust that the words spoken here by the masters are the highest truth, and I am excited to be bringing these important messages to the world at this time.

The messages within these pages are simple, and many are repeated by the masters over and over. They dispel many fallacies that man has chosen to believe and that have become part of his religions. When you read them, your beliefs may be challenged. The masters ask that you open your heart and mind to the possibilities and realities that are presented to you, and to cross the boundaries of the limiting beliefs that have held mankind back for so long. Mother Earth is on the brink of a new age, and it is time the world knew the truth.

I am ever grateful to Creator and the masters for their patience and their faith in me, and I thank them for trusting me to bring this book to the world.

I hope that the messages in this book resonate with you as much as they do with me.

Blessings and light,
Victoria Cochrane

(Note: I acknowledge that the Creator of All That Is embodies both the masculine and feminine, but for the purposes of consistency, all references to the Creator in this book are in the masculine.)

PART ONE

THE HIGHEST TRUTH: MASTER SAINT ALOYSIUS

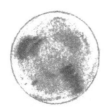

The Creator of All That Is

Wisdom is not written. Wisdom is just known. It comes from the ages and speaks the truth. We know what we know because we have lived it. We have seen it for ourselves.

Knowledge comes from our Creator, who knows all there is to know. It is freely given to us and is to be used with our free will for the highest and best intentions. The Creator loves us unconditionally. There is no room for judgement and condemnation, for the very essence of him is love. That is all there is.

You can feel him in your heart space. He is in every part of you. Every breath that you take is at one with the Creator. Nothing is separate from him. He has never left you, and he has never stopped loving you.

This is the highest truth. Let no man tell you that God does not love you or that God will strike you down with no mercy. The universe has been made on the promise of love and love only. Free will allows man to feel hatred and to seek vengeance on his fellow man, but do not allow him to tell you it is on God's behalf that he wreaks his wrath.

Let God wrap his love around you like a blanket. Feel it in your veins. He whispers in the trees and he loves you like a child. You are his child. Know that he is with you and a part of you. When you are one with God, you are one with the All. When you know this, when you truly know it, you will know and speak only of love. That is all.

I am God, the Creator.
I love you.
It is so.

The Sacredness of Life

All life is sacred. Mother Earth gives life and protects all of her children. The trees are the keepers of the Earth. They stand like sentries and hold guard for decades and centuries, knowing Mother Earth's secrets and keeping them safe. The tree sprites, nymphs, and fairies are the essence of nature. They guard the waterways, the plants, and the trees. They hold the energy of the Earth and sprinkle it with their magic. Fairies are what bring nature to life—they are the colours of the grass, of the flowers, and of the water. They are the tinkle of the stream and the call of the birds. They are the joy of the day and the magic of the night. They love life, and they bring their harmonies to all things that are of the Earth. They live in the sacredness, and they hold that energy for all things.

All living things have been created as sacred and perfect in the eyes of the Creator. No living thing is less important than the other. All is created as equal. Man is of no more importance than his cat or the tree on the hill. All is sacred; all is one. Man must love all things equally, and when he does, he will no longer feel that he needs to rule or possess. Mother Earth gives of her treasures freely. She has provided all that any life needs to be sustained while it is alive. But man has taken advantage of this gift, to the detriment of other life. He feels he must be the best, dominate, and rule. Sacred life is squandered, and Mother Earth dies.

A new chance awaits as Mother Earth prepares to ascend and take all life with her. Mother Earth holds all life in the bosom of her love, and she promises that all will come to those who cherish their lives as she does. For when we show love for the Earth, when we hold the Earth as sacred, we show love for ourselves, and we hold ourselves as sacred. We allow ourselves to be cherished, nurtured, and loved as completely as Mother Earth does and as God does. All is one. One is the *all*. That is all.

SAFE

The world is safe—it has been saved. The war has been won. It is only a matter of time before the whole world knows peace and love and the destruction of the past is behind us.

There are many happenings on Earth that are a result of decisions made in haste, lust, and greed. Yet there are many more that have more sinister undertones. The work of the dark forces cannot be undone, yet the light from the lightworkers of the world has greatly assisted in transmuting the intentions of these forces into events with lesser degrees of impact than were originally intended.

Let only love hold the space in your hearts and minds. Your thoughts must be centred on giving of yourself to others in service and with the highest and best of intentions. What serves the world will serve you, not the other way around. Ego has been the dominant force on Earth for far too long. When you let love take over, all will fall into place. The world as God intended will be restored, and the world will be at peace once again.

It will not be long before the world knows this. In fact, those of you reading this message may already do so. Be still and hear God's message. Hear him speak to you as a Father/Mother. You are loved, cherished, nurtured and cared for. You lessons are sanctioned, and the promises made to you are unbroken. Feel his love filling your heart and feeding your spirit. Know that when you rest in him, all will be well.

Mother Earth turns and will continue to do so, but she will be a new mother. She will be more vibrant, more stable, more radiant, and more dormant. Her hills will be aglow with the radiance of a new dawn, and her skies will be clearer than they have been for many a century.

Fear has been the main construct of man's mind for the longest time. The controlling forces of fear have kept him a puppet to materialism and to greed. He has not been able to speak his own mind or to stand in his power as a master or a servant, yet he has been a slave to the forces who silently and malevolently wielded their power. He has been controlled, manipulated, and forced to suffer unspeakable inhumanities by those who would hold the dominions of power and control of the Earth. This has now come to an end.

It will take some time to rid the Earth of all the hatred, greed, and lust for power that has been widespread. Even though ascension will be a force of reckoning for many, the energies of the Earth will be renewing for the next year. Take your time to adjust. Feel the new energy flow through your veins. Know that this new age of love and peace that has lain dormant within you is now awakening you to your true self: one of acceptance, love, and a oneness with God that you have long forgotten but will know henceforth as the only way to live, to know God, and to know yourself.

Peace comes in all forms but is only of the best intentions when it comes from a place of love and harmony. Many people live peaceful lives in service to themselves, and others live peaceful lives in service to others. The true meaning of peace comes from within. It is a true union between one's soul and the Creator. It is a love and acceptance of themselves in spirit as well as themselves as their human representations on Earth. When you accept who you are, that you are perfect in every way with nothing to be sorry for, will you truly know peace.

The world will know peace when humans are at peace with themselves, for the oneness they know with God, the Creator, will bring only love to their hearts. The true meaning of peace is love for oneself away from the world and in total oneness with God.

That is all.

Unspoken Truths

I speak now of the hidden truths and meanings of the Holy Bible. The New Testament was scribed by those who knew Jesus or by those who had links to them. Many of the chapters in the Bible are just letters or stories told to others but have since been taken to be truth. They have become part of a document that has been taken too literally as the indisputable word of God.

God speaks to man and through man, whose words and deeds can reflect or deflect God's truth. Man chooses how he interprets words spoken as God's words. The interpretation of these words has led to many untruths being upheld by religions around the world as gospel. It is time for these mistruths to be dispelled.

The word of God is love. God speaks only of love. His begotten son, Jeshua ben Joseph, was deemed as the saviour, and indeed, his coming awoke man to the presence of God and to the magic of his light and love.

God asks that the words spoken in the Bible be seen for what they are: representations of a time when thoughts and deeds were seen as representations of God's will. It was a time when the church took the coming of Jesus as its own and turned it into the only way to know God—the only way to think, act, and live eternal life. This is a nonsense. Jesus will willingly lead you to God's love, but he is *not* God himself. God is not a religion: God is love, and he is also man. God is life itself. He is in man—the air he breathes and the life he lives. To know and love yourself is to know and love God. Jeshua is a way, but he is not the only way. If you are lost he will lead you, but do not worship Jesus. Love and respect him. Talk to him and join with him in worshipping the Creator. When you do that, you will know oneness and peace. You will truly know love, and you will truly know yourself.

These are the unspoken truths.

To know the truth is to know God. Our God, the Creator, speaks only the truth. He does not lie or speak fallacies to stroke the ego. He speaks plainly and simply to the heart, not the mind. When you accept the truth, you are in divine union with God. All else will flow. There is no hiding from truth, for it cannot be undone. When you hide from truth you put into place a series of karmic steps that will lead you full circle back to what matters the most: the truth.

Facing truths is a hard lesson for many who have tried to cover their tracks with lies. Free will allows man to make choices that he deems are for his highest and best when, in fact, they hide who he really is—not only from others, but mostly from himself. When we deny ourselves, we deny God. We see ourselves as shadows of our true selves. We shine a light that is false. Yet others may see this and shy away, knowing that the person who speaks is not the person who is.

Know your truth and speak it. Do not speak it with judgement or condemnation; rather, speak it with love and tolerance. You are the perfect image of God in your own right. Shine your light from your divine heart. Love yourself for who you are.

You chose this.

You are living it. This is your truth. Be proud.

Love is all there is.

And so it is.

The Dawning of Ages

Take a moment to consider how the world was born. The Bible will tell you that God made the world in one week, but this is a fallacy. God held the intention that worlds would be created where life could take form—a place where souls could reside to live in harmony, learn their lessons, and evolve in their spiritual form.

Many worlds were created, but their physical forms took many eons to evolve. The evolution of man on Earth was a natural progression from ape to human. This was deliberate. One cannot evolve without learning lessons. One cannot gain knowledge if there are no lessons to learn. As one learns, one grows—not just in wisdom, but also in form.

Many millions and billions of years have passed in cycles of life and time. Many lessons have been learned, but many have also been spurned. The Earth has come to ascension to bring man back to his roots of unconditional love and absolute truth. There is no room for anger or retribution, as it will only serve to bring man back to Third Dimensional vibrations. Mother Earth is raising herself and all who accompany her to a Fifth Dimensional level. It is simply time to do so.

Life on Earth is no accident. It was designed and created by God to live in perfect harmony and synchronicity. As one species evolves, another follows, so that all life can live perfectly in tune with Mother Earth without any need to change or destroy it.

Change brings evolution, and evolution brings change. The design of the universe is of perfect synchronicity, love, and harmony. Free will is based on ego, which can be destructive and soul destroying. When ego is allowed to rule the world of man, the balance of harmony and synchronicity is changed, and this is not always for the better.

God is still creating, because man is a creator. God and man are one with one another and cannot be separated. The equilibrium of the creation of the universe will once again be restored.

Heed this message. Create with love. Use your ego for good, not self. Own your part of the evolution of Earth.

This is the highest truth.

And so it is.

Illumination

We bring forth the good news that the world is ablaze with light. Our God, the Creator, shines his light down upon the Earth and fills you all with his love and blessings. All you need to do is to open your heart to receive it, and you will also be ablaze.

When you are willing to open your heart to receive the light and love of God, you will know oneness with him. There will be no more feelings of separation or doom, for you will know what it is to have faith and trust without needing to worry about the future.

God gives of his love freely so that you, in turn, can shine it from your heart space out into the world. There is no other love but the love of God the Creator. When you love with your heart, you love with God's heart. When you shine your light, you are shining the light of God. God's light shines on the world and surrounds the Earth like a blanket. For those of you who already know what it is to love as God loves, shine your light on others. Show them the many blessings that come with knowing that all God requires is for man to love himself and others without restraint, judgement, condemnation, or barriers.

There are no restrictions on love; that is all there is. There are no boundaries or conditions on God's love. Religion is only required when one can find no other way to God's heart. If you have lost your way, Jesus will shine his light like a beacon and lead you to him, for he will always be there, ready and waiting, joyously welcoming you into the light. Then you will know peace without restrictions.

You will know God. You will know yourself.

You are one.

That is all.

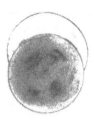

Ascended Masters

Masters are the keepers of the universe and its knowledge. They are the flame that keeps that knowledge alive. Masters have lived many lives and learned many lessons, which they pass on to masters on both the ethereal and human planes.

Ascended Masters reside on the Upper Fifth Plane of Existence. They have ascended there through many lifetimes and by always being in service to God and to man. They know only love and feel only goodness in their hearts. Masters can teach you much, but they are also still learning themselves. They are grounded through the human body, and their work is manifested through the work of lightworkers on Earth. In some respects they are the behind-the-scenes workers who do their work tirelessly and for the greater good.

There are many Ascended Masters who still walk this Earth. The time that it takes to be born, to grow, and then to be awakened is offset by the coming to Earth of many Ascended Masters who have chosen to reincarnate for the benefit of the planet and of mankind. Many babies are of higher energies who have been here many times before. They know their way around, and they have much knowledge to impart. Their eyes hold the depth of their connection to Source and of the goodness in their hearts. They have much to teach and more to learn. They are the way-showers of the world, and they must be honoured for the lessons they bring.

The life of the Master on the Earthly Plane can be fraught with trauma and pain. Many higher energies who choose to come to Earth for the greater good find that the denseness of the energy is too great for them to handle, and they leave earlier than was intended. This is their choice, for which they must not be judged. It is the way of the world to manipulate those who give of their energy freely, and the condemnation of the world is an injustice to which the Master is unaccustomed. Many Masters choose harsh lessons on Earth so they may use this knowledge to benefit others. It is always harder in reality than it was in the planning. They know this, but the nature of the energy on Earth leaves them with little defences to fight the strong urges of the ego and of the materialism that is the plague of the human existence.

Judge not of what you know little about. Know that in all things there are lessons to be learned, and Masters must also learn them. The Masters who choose to stay in the ethereal realms are there to support, guide, and counsel those who are back on Earth. It is a symbiotic relationship that is essential to the health and well-being of the Earth-bound master. Those who have lost their way have usually lost their connection to their spiritual advisors and to Source. When this is reconnected they find their way and rediscover their life's purpose.

Many of those who have been awakened are now assisting those who have lost their way to rediscover the reasons they reincarnated back to Earth. This task is of the utmost importance, because it brings back into balance that which has been lost and forgotten. Many of you are noticing the awakening of those who have before been in slumber. The time is nigh for the awakening of the Earth and its Masters. This is a time of rejoicing and rediscovering. The veil is lifting, and for good reason.

Creator calls you to your purpose, and you will answer because that is why you are here. Mother Earth rejoices, and her sigh reverberates around the world and into the universe. We are reunited as one.

And so it is.

Blessings

We have bestowed upon the Earth the blessings of love and commitment. We are the Great Brotherhood of Light, now known as the Cosmic Council. We are ever present and ever vigilant in our fight for peace on the Earth. We shine our light and join our love with the lightworkers present on the Earthly Plane at this time. We protect them and assist them as they continue their work for Mother Earth.

Many years ago a major battle began on the Astral Plane. There was much disruption to the energy patterns on the Earth. Darker forces who wish to rule and dominate the Earth have been fighting for control using any means available to them. They cannot win. They have not won.

The Great Brotherhood of Light has been a major force to be reckoned with. Our vigilance has led the many lightworkers who have answered the call to unite in light and love to combat the darker forces and to weaken their defences. Mother Earth is grateful for this respite, but she is also weakened. She cannot sustain the battle or the negativity that has flowed onto the human race any longer. It is time to ascend and to leave the battle behind.

We are the lightworkers of the Etheric Realm. We are the Masters of the highest order who answer to God, our Creator, and only to him. Our love is his love, our light is his light, and we shine it to all who wish to receive it.

Light and dark are not opposites. They are merely a gradient on a scale that symbolises one's chosen path of learning. We cannot make you choose the light, but we can tell you that all paths lead there—it is just a matter of time. How long it takes you to get there is totally up to you. For, if you choose the long way, it is not the wrong way; it will just be the harder path of lessons that will still lead you to God in the end. It cannot be any other way.

We will lead you to the light. Let us do so. When you live in the light, you know only love.

We are one.

And so it is.

Lessons

All life is a lesson. The lessons we learn help us to evolve spiritually, but humans can grow as humans using life's lessons as well. This all leads to evolvement of the soul. Lessons are chosen according to our soul journey. We choose our lessons to help us to grow. Not all lessons are easy, and not all will lead to resolutions. Sometimes there is karmic intervention to our lessons, and sometimes our lessons are as a result of karma.

We cannot evolve without learning, but lessons are only learnt when we have accepted their consequences. Acceptance brings peace within ourselves and a knowing that this experience has led to a greater understanding of the world and our place in it. It also leads to a better understanding of the impact we have on the world and its consequences. If we choose not to learn our lessons, we will invoke the cycle of reincarnation so that we have another opportunity to learn them. A lesson the second time around is a brave choice, because the situation you find yourself in may be one of great hardship and uncertainty.

Choose your lessons well and learn them as you live them, so your soul will know great growth and evolvement, leading to wisdom and truth. The truth can hurt the ego, and it can also uplift it. The lesson of life will always lead to oneness with God and an acceptance of self, a knowing of one's own truth and a love for life as it is. A sense of completion and fulfilment will follow in life after death as one's soul recognises the lesson that has been learned and uses this wisdom to benefit others. When one can use the wisdom gained to teach in service to others, one has gained Mastery.

Learn and accept your lessons. Know that you chose to learn them. In every situation, ask yourself, "What is the lesson to be learned here?" Then you will know your higher self and your higher truth, and you will be on your path—the one you chose, and the one you designed in oneness with God our Creator.

And so it is.

Deliverance

It is not for God to deliver you from sins, for you have not sinned. You have merely been learning the lessons you have chosen to learn and exerting your free will as you journey upon your path. Your free will is yours alone, allowing you to choose the way in which you learn your lessons and the length that your lessons will be. No choice is wrong, but some choices will lead you to Mastery sooner, which is the way of enlightenment of the soul.

Christ came to Earth to deliver man from sin. His suffering was felt upon the Earth and around the world. He knew his destiny, he knew of his fate, yet he took on this task willingly, knowing that the way he showed to all mankind was the path that leads to God and enlightenment. It is the path of choice, but it is also our own destiny that we have chosen in oneness and communion with God. There is nothing to be forgiven, for each path is one of learning that takes us down a certain road. Whether we invoke karma is up to the invocation of our free will and must be reckoned with by our soul at a later time.

You do not need forgiveness for that which you have chosen to learn. The stage of Earth is where you play out your lessons and where your soul evolves. The stage can at times be brutal and realities harsh. Other souls who are also enacting their lessons get caught up in the dramas, and the reason you are learning the lessons may seem lost to you. Keep in mind that everything that happens on the Earthly Plane is an illusion. Your every move has been orchestrated by you before you were born. The time of your birth, the family you would be born into, the type of life you had and the lessons you would learn. You also chose the method and time of your death according to your previous life contracts and karma that you needed to repay or that needed to be repaid to you. What seems like a tragedy or a travesty on Earth is rarely so; the dramas that play out are merely humans learning their lessons and enacting out their life's contract—the one they made and agreed upon before they were born. So you see, dear ones, that the harsh realities of Earth are lessons of the soul and therefore do not need forgiveness. You must rid yourself of guilt and make peace with your soul. Any repercussions that come from your fellow humans as a result of your actions are an invocation of the Law of Karma, and will also lead to further soul growth and evolvement.

The realities of life as a human on Earth cannot be downplayed by those of us in the Etheric Realms who are watching it unfold. We honour those who have chosen to incarnate on the Earthly Plane, for we know the difficulties and we feel your pain. Do not think that we do not notice what you do as a human on Earth, but it is how you integrate your lessons into your soul journey that is of the utmost importance.

Pure light and love come only from God, and each man is made in God's image. The guilt you may feel at the deeds you have done is a part of your soul growth and needs no forgiveness from God, because God knows your path and he sees your growth. He knows your truth. He guides you and speaks to you from the heart, telling you that he loves you and that he knows the real you. He knows you as innately good. He sees you as he created you—perfect in every way.

Deliverance comes with forgiveness, but again this does not need to come from God. He sees you with love. He leads you down the path of learning with light in his eyes. He says, "You are already forgiven, my child. You have done this deed so you may know in your heart where the true meaning lies. When you can forgive yourself, true deliverance will come. This will bring true resolution and redemption."

The deeds that have brought Mother Earth to ascension are not the result of free will alone. Dark forces have kept the ego at the forefront of man's consciousness. Man has been a puppet at the hands of a manipulator so strong in his power that no pure consciousness could find its way through. But man is awakening to a new age. He sees the deeds he has done and he no longer sees a reason for them. War has lost all meaning, and hatred leads to nowhere but darkness. He sees a way to make things right, and he refuses to listen to any more lies.

God's light is the way to freedom. When you live in the light, there is nothing to forgive. You see past mistakes as lessons in the making, and you are wiser for them. Love is the way to forgiveness. It is the way to the light and freedom from the weight of the past.

You are forgiven. You are delivered. Mother Earth is ascending, and the way is clear to use the lessons of the past to build a new future: a future of living in the light and knowing that your life is where it should be; in the moment, one with God, Mother Earth, and each other. Be true to yourself and be free of guilt, for there is no sin, and nothing to forgive. The deeds you have done against other men will indeed be reckoned with when your soul leaves the Earthly Plane. You may need to reincarnate again to play out the karma you have invoked upon others. This is part of your soul journey, and all lessons lead to the light, even when they have originated from darkness.

You are a child of God, and loved in every way.

Know this, and you will know God. Know this and you will also know yourself.

You are one.

And so it is.

Babylon

The ancient gardens of Babylon have been fabled many times and are renowned for their beauty and history. The site where they once were has been destroyed many times over, but the symbolism of their creation is of importance. Never before had something so beautiful or magnificent in structure been attempted, and the feat of their construction was celebrated far and wide.

The reason for this chapter is to remind you that gardens must be tended and nurtured for them to flourish and grow. Every human life is like the Hanging Gardens of Babylon: magnificent in structure, but vulnerable in nature. If human life is not nurtured it will die. Humans, unlike plants, need much more than water to thrive and grow. Yes, they need food, but they also need love, a sense of belonging, and a feeling of destiny and purpose. If they do not receive or feel those things, their spirits will be damaged, and they will lose their way.

God is the gardener of the human spirit. He nurtures it and tends to it, lavishing it with love and belonging. He tells each and every one of you that he is here to look after you and to help you to find your way. Without God to guide us we are lost. If we do not feel him with us, we feel no sense of belonging, and our spirits begin to wither. We feel as though something is missing, but we cannot identify what it is. As full as our lives may be and as busy as we are, there is still something missing. We have lost our gardener.

Love is the food of the soul. It is the way to God, our Creator, and the way to our own hearts. When we are in love or feel loved, we blossom like a flower in the rain. We grow in self, and we give of ourselves to others. We feed each other with love and friendship. We are flowers together in the garden of life.

Tend to your garden with God's love. Let his light fall down upon you like rain. Feel the warmth of his love like the sun. He will open your hearts to the glorious feeling of belonging and of being nurtured. When you can do this, you will feel love for yourself and love for those around you. You will see that everything on Earth is connected and reliant on each other. You will feel, indeed, like you are in a magnificent garden where everything grows, blooms, and gives joy. There is no better place than God's garden.

Join him.

We are one.

It is so.

Deity

God is the Creator of the universe. He is one with the *all*. He is in every particle and in every breath. He is ancient and wise, yet he is ever new. Creator speaks with love and compassion, but he does not let emotions rule his words. His heart speaks only love, but his words are divine wisdom and truth. He will never waver from truth and will never speak falsehoods. God rules but he does not control. He leads but he does not force. He guides, but obedience to God is a choice, not a mandate.

Love is all there is. This has been spoken of throughout this book, and when it is heeded the world will truly change. God is not a persecutor, nor is he judge or jury. He is not a sage who speaks of one wisdom or one way. He calls you by name and he knows every heart. He shows you his way, but he does not make you choose him. He is there for you always, even when you have turned your back. When you finally come home to him, he is there with open arms and joy in his heart.

God is you. You are God. There is no separation. You are one with him. When you know God, you know yourself. When you love yourself, you love God. Anything that you do on Earth is between you and God only. Let no man tell you what is right or wrong, because the lessons you are learning have been chosen by you and ordained by God. However, the judgement you receive on Earth from man for deeds you may have done against another are a result of karma, and the consequences must be borne on the Earthly Plane.

There is no other way to the light than love. Love will lead you to God's light as sure as the sun is beating down on the Earth. Replace all anger, frustration, hatred, and hurt with love, and you have found God. It is that simple.

Man has found religion, and he has found war. He has used his ego to make decisions that have wreaked havoc on Mother Earth. There is no going back from these things, yet the way forward is to forgive yourself and commit to loving God and loving yourself. When you can do that all else will flow. Divine flow is the seed of creation. When you allow, trust, and have faith that all is in divine timing and as it should be, then the law of abundance will be activated. You can manifest anything you wish, negative or positive, with the thoughts you think and the beliefs you hold. When you can change these for the better, you manifest great abundance in your life. All creation flows through love, and love is the way of Christ and the way to God. There is nothing more. Why make it hard on yourself? Think good thoughts, and only goodness can come. Think bad thoughts, and that is what you will manifest.

God does not judge you. God does not condemn. He wishes only for you to feel love in your hearts and the best of each other. He is the way to truth, love, and light.

That is all.

And so it is.

Part Two

Messages from the Masters

THE GREATER GOOD

Merlin Speaks

I speak with you of the many blessings of the Earth. These days we speak of the doom and gloom of the Third Dimension, and it seems that ascension cannot come fast enough. Yet we must remember the many blessings that living in this dimension has brought and the lessons that you can take forward with you to the Fifth Dimension.

Everything happens for a reason. There are no coincidences. Man was made with an ego so that he could learn how difficult it is to balance the ego mind with the spiritual body. In spirit, there is no ego. We live in peace and harmony. We love unconditionally. We judge nobody. We are in total balance and in total union with our Creator. There is not time or space to limit us, and no belief systems stall us. We have total faith, total trust, and total belief.

Yet when we incarnate into a human body, whether we are an Ascended Master or not, the force of the ego is one that is truly terrifying. We are consumed with want. We are consumed with desires to please our senses and our every need. We are consumed with ourselves, and the greater good of mankind, which was our intention to serve when we chose to be born, is forgotten.

As children, we still "see." We are still in communion with our Creator, and we are in tune with nature. We have wants, but many of us still know why we are here. As we grow, the indoctrination of society corrodes our seeing eye, and we are blinded to the glory and wonderment of creation.

You cannot evolve into a higher spiritual being without the lessons learned on the plane of the Earth. Evolvement depends on knowledge, and the wisdom gained through living in ego is invaluable to those who wish to lead in the etheric realms. The blessings come in the knowing that the lessons were not in vain, that the hard times and the good times were all leading to the evolvement of the spirit into a master of the highest order, and that this evolvement is to lead to the greater good of mankind.

Evolvement takes many lifetimes and many lessons. In between lifetimes, the healing, the learning, the discussions, and the teachings all lead to the evolvement of many, not just the soul who has learned the lessons. We all teach each other. We all work together to evolve to the highest order. We are one together.

Many of you on Earth are now realising that working together is the only way to achieve success, and that when knowledge is shared it leads to the greater good. As you do this, you move out of ego and into that space of joy. Knowing that you have helped someone move to a better place in their life will lead to evolvement of not just your soul, but theirs as well. What serves you serves others. Service is not a place of reckoning but a place of attainment. In service to others you are in service to God, and your soul will be rewarded with higher knowledge and wisdom that can be used for the greater good.

I am Merlin.

Ascension

Lord Melchizadek Speaks

The ascension of the world has occurred. Mother Earth has been preparing to ascend for some time. No longer can she sustain the corruption and greed of mankind or the negativity that envelops her like a cloak—she must shrug it off and ascend so that the future of the human race is assured. Much work has been done to ensure that ascension will happen, and on the 12/12/2012 it took place.

There are some on the Earth who will choose not to ascend with Mother Earth at this time. This is their choice. There is no judgement in this decision, for they exercise their free will. For those who choose to ascend, the time is ready for you to ensure your vibrations are of the highest order, for the energies associated with ascension from the Third to the Fifth Dimension are great. If you have not made the preparations for this moment, your body will experience sickness, dizziness, and aching, and you will find it much more difficult to assimilate the energy of the Fifth Dimension into your cells.

It is necessary now to activate your lightbodies so that you are vibrating at the frequency necessary to exist in the Fifth Dimensional frequencies. For those who have not yet had any chakra activations, I recommend that you exercise haste and begin them soon. People will need at least three activations to bring in their lightbodies, depending upon the frequency at which they are vibrating now. Some will require more than three.

As each activation takes place, your chakras will be activated to hold a higher and purer energy that is of light. Each chakra is aligned to a certain ray of light that is associated with an archangel of the Seven Rays. Each ray has its own particular frequency. To be vibrating at the optimum frequency of each ray, the chakra must be attuned using energy that is accorded by a master with the recipient's permission. The chakra will not be activated any higher than the person can cope with, according to the vibrations they are holding at the time. The clearer the person's chakra is, the higher it can be activated. Now is the time to be preparing your chakras to be attuned to the optimum frequencies, for the time of ascension grows close; for some, it has already occurred. We, the Masters, are here to help all humans to ascend in the manner that is most comfortable to the human body.

There are many lightworkers on Earth at this time who have agreed to be bridges for ascension. They will help people ready their bodies to accept the Fifth Dimensional frequencies. You will know who they are. They are bringers of the light, and we, the Masters, work through them. Allow them to help you, as the world stands ready to release negativity and go to the light.

When the Earth ascended, her darkness turned to light, and all of the energies of corruption were shaken. There is no room on the new Earth for darkness, as her vibrations are now too high. The new Earth will be one of love, harmony, and compassion. The world of nature will reverberate with joy as the Earth is renewed and becomes bountiful again. Everything will shine as it has not done for a long time. This will be the chance for mankind to step into a new age of love and peace, one that has been dreamt of but that he thought he could not achieve.

Time matters not in the moment of ascension, for it has been and it will be. It is over and it is yet to come. Some will know of the exact moment when they have ascended, and others will not feel it. Know that it will happen, and when it does, we are here to assist.

Feel into your heart to know the truth of your existence and of the essence of your soul. Look into the meaning of your life, and you will know what your purpose is in this lifetime. Strip away the past and see the future, but know that this moment is the one that matters the most. For you are loved more than you can imagine, and your footsteps upon this Earth are treasured.

Soon it will be.
It has already been.
Prepare, dear ones.
It is so.

The Lightbody

Lord Melchizadek Continues

The lightbody is activated when the chakras are attuned to a higher frequency.

Humans all vibrate at a certain frequency, and chakras are spinning in attunement and alignment with the body. When the chakras become sluggish or blocked, they lose their correct frequency, and the whole body becomes unbalanced. The light within each chakra is formatted within a certain ray that aligns to the frequency of an archangel. The colour of each chakra contains the frequency that is centred within one of those seven rays. Most people do not look after their chakras or are even aware of them, so they remain blocked and vibrate at a much lower frequency than is required to attain Fifth Dimensional vibrations.

Lightbody chakra activations are necessary to help bring the body in alignment with the seven rays and to allow the chakras to vibrate at the higher frequency that is necessary to anchor in the lightbody for ascension. The lightbody will assist you with assimilating into the much higher energies of the Fifth Dimension at the time of ascension. If your lightbody is not anchored in, you will experience disequilibrium and sickness for some time.

The lightbody is your etheric body. It is the state you were in before you were born. You were in total alignment with the seven rays and with Creator. You were in the light and of the light. The normal body vibrates at 390 megahertz for perfect health. The lightbody is vibrating at a much higher frequency; the chakras are rotating faster and are in total attunement and alignment with one another. The angelic frequency of the lightbody is is 525 megahertz, but humans cannot cope with a frequency so high.

When your lightbody is completely anchored, and the whole world has ascended, your body will be vibrating at 465 megahertz.

When a Master performs an activation through a lightworker, he can only activate each chakra to its highest frequency according to its current vibration. If it is blocked with discordant energy it will need to be cleared and will be less receptive to higher frequencies. That is why many people's chakras do not all activate to the same frequency in one session, because they have been vibrating at different frequencies that are not in alignment with one another or with the ray it is associated with. It may be necessary, therefore, to perform several activations to allow each activation to integrate and assimilate into the body. It will also avoid flooding the body with too much energy, which would also result in sickness.

The lightbody is aligned with the Crystalline Grid, which surrounds the Earth. It has the same pattern as the Crystalline Grid and is connected to it at all times. The diamond points of the lightbody align with the diamond points on the grid. When your lightbody is anchored in, you are also anchored into the Crystalline Grid, and your light becomes one with the grid and all other lightworkers. This is an important part of ascension, both for Mother Earth and for the humans choosing to ascend.

When you have anchored in your lightbody you will be vibrating at a higher frequency, and your thoughts will also be of a higher order. You may find that you no longer wish to associate with people whose thoughts and actions are not of integrity. You will be less likely to judge and condemn others and more likely to accept others for who they are, and you will find yourself persuading other people to do the same. Your body may need different food, and you will feel the need to find time for quiet contemplation, meditation, and prayer. Your spiritual gifts will be magnified, and your connection to God will feel complete.

This is a momentous time for the Earth, loved ones. Rejoice, and allow this to happen for the good of all.

And so it is.

THE CHRIST CONSCIOUSNESS

Jesus Speaks

Love is eternal and never-ending. Love is the flame that burns within the heart of our Creator, who loves all of his children as his own and who holds each one in perfection. His love brought me to Earth and sustained me through all of my days on Earth as a human being who lived in and for the light. My love is what holds me to the Earth in service still as I walk amongst you and bring you ever closer to the light of our Creator and my loving father.

My love is called the Christ Consciousness because it is the consciousness that binds the Earthly Plane to the light of the Seventh Plane, the Creator, our God. It is the bridge for the consciousness of man, so that he will know oneness with God as I have always known it. I am the bridge that avoids the separation between thought and deed on the Earthly Plane and that of our loving God, who has never left you and who will always love you, no matter what. There can be no separation from a part of you that lives and breathes as you live and breathe. When you love yourself, you love God, for you are one. If you have forgotten this, my love is the bridge that brings you back together. All paths lead to the light.

The infinity symbol is the symbol of the universe, which is vast and ever expanding. My love is like the universe: all-encompassing. It knows no beginning and no end. When you see this symbol, you can feel me with you. If you *ever* need me, for any reason, all you need to do is ask, dear ones. I will always answer your call.

The universe cannot exist without love.: it is simply not possible. When you open your hearts to the reality that only love is real, you will know the Christ Consciousness, and you will have accepted oneness. All paths lead to the light, and some paths are longer than others. When you choose me as your path, the way is short. My Father knows best. He knew where my birth and death would lead. I also knew, and I accepted the task willingly. There can be no other road to take than the road that leads to the unity of man with God through the Christ Consciousness. It has already happened. We are there, and how glorious it is.

So be it.

Living in the Light

Jesus Continues

The light is ever present. It lives and breathes through you and other humans whose intentions towards others and the planet are pure. Know this: the work that the lightworkers do on Earth is no trivial matter. Every time they send healing energy to the planet from their heart space, the timeline, the Crystalline Grid, or the Seventh Plane, which is the Creator, they are magnifying the possibilities and opportunities for people who are still living in Third Dimensional energy.

The universe is an open channel, as are lightworkers and anyone who has opened their crown chakra to receive the light. If you allow this wonderful gift for receiving our messages to be blocked by doubt and fear, the opportunities for communication with us will be lost, and those whom you are helping will not benefit. Give all of your concerns to us and to God. Trust, have faith, and receive.

When you live in the light, the darkness fades and love becomes ever present. You will radiate light and love, and help raise the vibrations of the world simply by being there. People will be drawn to you and will find your presence healing and calming. They will come to you like moths to a flame, because your light will draw them in, heal them, and help them see that there are other ways of dealing with the problems of life rather than being immersed in negativity.

Look to Creator to bring his light through your crown chakra. Ask him to open up your third eye to allow you to "see" all that is open to you. Let him guide you to his light, with his light and to be in his light. Creator's light is love, and his love is unconditional. There is no other way to enlightenment than through living in God's light. His light will become your light, and you will lead the way. You will truly be a lightworker of God, for God, and with God, for you are one with God, whether you know it or not.

I am Jeshua-ben-Joseph

The Concept of Oneness

Jesus Continues

Let us take a moment to consider the Earth as we see her—as a pearl within an oyster. She is perfect in every way until the moment that the shell protecting her is opened and the outside world can come in. As she sits within her shell, closed to the world, with only water and nutrients allowed in, she contemplates perfection. She sees herself as the mother of all her children, who are also perfect in every way, hiding in their shells, protected and beautiful.

But there comes the day when man opens all of the shells and exposes the pearls to the elements and to his influences. The pearls are disrespected, treated roughly, and exploited for their beauty. They are sold to the highest bidder and worn as ornaments. They are often housed in drawers and containers and forgotten. They are separated from each other, never to be together again.

That is how God sees all of his children—as pearls within the oyster of his love. They are united as one, and separation is merely an illusion of man. As man goes about his life on Earth, he sees himself as separate from the Earth. The Earth is an oyster to be exploited, not cherished as he cherishes his own life and those of his loved ones. He also sees himself as separate from our Creator, who holds all life in the palm of his hand and nurtures it with loving intention.

No life is separate from God, because he has made all life in his image. All life is held in perfection and perfect oneness with God and itself. You cannot live separately from God without creating the illusion that nothing is sacred. All life and elements on Earth were created as sacred by Creator. When you live the illusion of separateness, you lose your ability to sense your own worth. You lose respect for yourselves and the pearl that Mother Earth really is.

You are the pearls within God's love, which is your oyster! The world is a pearl itself, because it has never lost sight of itself as perfection. Human life and Mother Earth are not separate from each other! They all form the perfect pearl held within God's love. Until this is realised, dear ones, Mother Earth will continue to suffer at the hands of those who cannot grasp the concept of oneness. Ascension will work its magic for a time, but we must work hard to teach this concept to others. It is the only hope of staying in the Fifth Dimension indefinitely.

And so it is.

Religion

Mother Mary Speaks

Wisdom is a great teacher. It speaks to us from the ages, and from the lessons we have learned across many lifetimes. We cannot dispute the teachings of our elders, but we can add to universal knowledge through our own learnings.

I speak to you today of times past, when man learned his lessons well and applied them in ways that benefited all of mankind, when men and women lived off the land and shared all of their resources, but gave back to the land as much as they took. The Earth was their temple and the heavens their master. There have been a few times since when the good of all has overcome selfishness and greed, but those times have been short-lived.

The ego of man and the desires that overcome it have meant that the lessons of the past have not been retained. We cannot undo the mistakes man has made in the name of God and of my son Jeshua. As well-intentioned as they may seem, there has been much damage done and many untruths spoken in the name of religion that were never so and never meant for the consciousness of man.

My son is the son of God. He is pure light and love. He is the way to God that is true. He spoke of love in no ways that man had ever heard, and many men have heeded his call. Religion has served man for a time, bringing him some peace and reconciliation with our Creator. But Jeshua's sacrifice has been misunderstood, and he has been idolised when that was never the intention. All glory must go to God; Jeshua is merely the conduit for Creator's love. Man has spent too long revering Christ for the sacrifice he made. It is time to step out of the past and look to the future, for the *second coming* is not what the human race has interpreted it to be. Christ walks amongst all of you every day because he is *in* all of you every day. There is no separation from God, and there can be no separation from the Christ Consciousness.

Jeshua's sacrifice has done its work. It has embedded his love into all things, including plants, animals, and humans. You cannot walk the Earth and feel love without my Jeshua permeating every part of your being. It is simply not possible.

Religion has played its part but it does have a lot to answer for. The Church has actively taught separation, while Jeshua actively teaches oneness. The Church has rebuked sexual intercourse, while Jeshua shows us that it is the way to the light. Through the union with your twin flame, who has never left you, you will bring wholeness and oneness to the Earth, and separation will be a thing of the past. The Church and its religions have brought judgement, hatred, separatism, and violence. It has divided the world and caused war and uprising. The sacrifice that Jeshua made is a mockery in the face of such adversity and scorn. Where is the love in such actions? How can we ever make peace with God if we cannot make peace with ourselves? You are made in God's image, and you are one with God. That has never changed, although your actions defy this.

Love was never meant to hurt or harm. It was never meant to be a judgement or condemnation. It is not a competition or a race. Love simply is. When you embrace love, you embrace God, and with that action you acknowledge that Jeshua is part of your life and forever in your heart. For that to be you need no religion. Let it just be.

And so it is.

THE VIOLET FLAME

Saint Germaine Speaks

The Violet Flame comes to us as a gift from Mother Earth. It is freely given to transmute all negativity to positive energy. Mother Earth needs all lightworkers to utilise the flame as part of their healing energy, as it will greatly assist in her ascension.

The Violet Flame is of no substance; rather, it is pure energy that is angelic in nature. It has healing properties that can be used by those with the highest and best intentions. It springs from eternal love from Creator, our God, and is sourced from Mother Earth's diamond core. It is the sacred element of fire, but it carries no heat. Say its name, hold it with intention, and send it with love.

Archangel Zadkiel is the true keeper of the Violet Flame. His wife, Holy Amethyst, transmits this energy through her work with the crystal form, amethyst. Together they coordinate the provision of the flame to masters and lightworkers around the world. There are many masters who are willing to share the flame to those who are deserving, for it is of the utmost urgency that the flame envelops the Earth. Sanctus Germanis (Saint Germaine), Archangel Michael, Lady Nada, Joseph, Christopher Columbus, Buddha, Jesus, Mary Magdalene, Mother Mary, and Kuan Yin are all Masters who can pass on the flame to others. There are other Masters who can also do this—all you need do is ask.

Do not hold the flame in contempt or consider that it is of no use or purpose. Its gift to the world is in its ability to inflict no pain but to bring resolution and peace. It transmutes all anger, aggression, sadness, grief, agony, and pain to positive energy. Its effect is immediate. Know that this gift is freely available to those of the highest order whose work is selfless and for the benefit of others. Those who know not of this power can be beneficiaries by those who call upon it to heal and transform. Its nature is pure. Its energy is sacred. It is a gift from this world but not of this world. Using the Violet Flame will raise the energies of those on the planet who know no other means. It is of the utmost urgency that this be done.

And so it is.

The Four Sacred Elements

WATER

Master Aloysius Speaks

Water is sacred. It surrounds the Earth with its blessings. It gives life to many things. It is both fluid and solid. It is a mixture of oxygen and hydrogen, with a dose of minerals in different quantities, depending on its source. Water takes on the form of whatever is holding it. It can also form crystals, and it can wear away rocks. Therefore, it is a powerful force of which time is no master.

Water holds memories. The past is held in the waters of the Earth to be accessed by man if he so wishes. It is a keeper of the Violet Flame and a holder of many secrets. Water washes away sins and it cleanses the soul. It is vibrant and youthful, even though it is ancient. Water is sacred because it comes from the bosom of Mother Earth. It is in her keeping. Water is the fabric that holds the world together; lands are joined by great bodies of water that cross the world and unite it. Water is to be held in awe and revered, because it is a life-force of the Earth.

To hold a fear of water is not to fear life itself, but it is to lack a respect for all that is sacred. Man cannot rule water any more than he can rule the Earth. When he uses water or anything from the land, he is entering into an agreement that he will cherish it and respect it. If he chooses not to then he is lacking respect for the sacredness of the land, of the water, and of the Earth from which he draws the water. Water is sacred. Man needs water to survive, so man is also sacred. Therefore, when he disrespects water, he also disrespects himself.

CRYSTALS

Master Aloysius Continues

Crystals are of the Earth, but they need water to form. They form over many years and can take decades or even centuries to grow to full form. Crystals are as sacred as the Earth and water that form them, and they are the home for many living creatures that reside within them. They are the salt of the Earth and the blessings of the Earth.

Crystals have many healing properties and can benefit man if they are treated with the utmost care and respect. They all resonate at a certain frequency, so they can be used for different purposes at different times. Some crystals work together, and some work against each other, but when used in harmony with one another, the healing energy is magnified and can speed up the healing process. Only wash crystals in the purest of water and keep them in a place out of harm's way. Crystals will serve you when you have the highest and best respect for them and intentions for the healing to be done.

Many of the crystals within Mother Earth have been there for all time and are the energy that the Earth is built around. They vibrate at a frequency that resonates with the other six planes of existence and that keeps everything in balance. When their vibrations are altered, it affects all of the other planes and the life that dwells within them. That is why so much frenetic energy can build up on the Earth if the resonance of the vibrations is off kilter. Harmonious balance within and between the planes is of the utmost importance to maintain the state of equilibrium.

I implore the lightworkers of the world to join with the Masters of the Etheric Realms each day to send balancing energy to the crystals within Mother Earth. This can be done by sending energy through intention from your heart space. You can tap into the frequencies of the crystals by humming a tone in your head with your hand on your heart space. Keep your intentions on the crystals and on balancing their vibrations to be one with Mother Earth. Ask us to help you, and the energy will be magnified. If you maintain this for up to five minutes each day, you will be doing Mother Earth and all who dwell upon her a great service.

    I thank you.

Amethyst Crystals and the Violet Flame

Holy Amethyst Speaks

Use amethyst crystals to absorb negative energies. Amethyst has many healing properties. It will also protect your aura from absorbing other people's energies. Amethyst crystals have long been used in this way, but their healing properties are lesser known.

Know that the Violet Flame does not come from the amethyst crystal, yet it contains many healing properties that are akin to its own. When you use them in tandem for your healings, both for Mother Earth and for human needs, the combination will be a powerful one.

To combine amethyst crystals with the Violet Flame, all you need do is hold the crystal in your palm as you invoke the flame. The properties of the crystal will be combined with the flame as you send healing. This will be most beneficial. I recommend you make it a regular part of your practice.

Love and blessings.

Fire

Saint Germaine Speaks

Fire is sacred. It burns ever eternal within Mother Earth. It is one of the four sacred elements. The sacredness of fire is not in its ability to control or be controlled, but in its connection to the earth and in its reliance on air, which is a sacred element. Hold it in awe, not in fear, for when it is feared it can be used against you by those who wish you harm. I am not speaking only of humans, but of the darker forces that wish to rule and control.

Stop to think of your memories of fire. They would mostly be ones of light, warmth, and comfort. But if you have suffered burns, loss of property, or loss of life, fire will hold you to ransom. Fire cannot really be tamed, for it will always lose—or take—control if given the opportunity. Fire can be controlled just as humans can feel controlled by the elements and by each other.

Fire needs a healthy respect. It will do your bidding if you treat it wisely. If you fear fire, you fear control. Perhaps you are actually feeling controlled. If you have no fear of fire, you have no fear of control, but perhaps you also cannot be controlled or are out of control. If you respect fire, you also respect yourself. We cannot always control the elements, but we can treat them respectfully, which means we can benefit from them without coming to any harm. We can also use them to help ourselves, each other and Mother Earth.

The Sacred Fire within each and every one of you burns with an eternal flame. This fire holds you to the Etheric Realms and is your connection to Spirit and to the Creator, your God. The Sacred Fire burns within you and keeps your love for Creator and for yourself holy, sacred and pure. If you have lost the love for yourself or for God, then your Sacred Fire burns low. Know that it will never, and cannot, be extinguished, but if it has lost its brightness, you will feel lost and disconnected. Love for God is something that all humans have within them whether they are religious in this life or not. Holy fire burns within you all, for you are all holy, all one with the Creator and all creators in your own right. As you are one, losing love for God will also result in the loss of love and respect for yourself.

Look into your Sacred Heart Centre and fuel the Sacred Fire that burns within you. Feed it by feeling Creator's love within you, surrounding you and giving you life. Creator's love is the oxygen that feeds your Sacred Fire. Know that his love is never-ending and all-encompassing. It will keep the Sacred Fire within you burning brightly, keeping you warm and allowing you to hold the light like a beacon for others.

Know this, for this is the highest truth.

EARTH

Mother Earth Speaks

Earth is the foundation of the world. It is what sustains life. It carries the DNA of all life structures on Earth.

The Earth is connected to all things, all life, all thoughts, actions, words, and cosmic forces. It is separate from nothing. There is nothing that the Earth does not know, feel, or interpret. I am Mother Earth; I am whole and I am universal. I am the mother of all life. I love all of my children, but I am sad. I feel I have been abandoned by my children as you go your separate ways and make decisions that are not for my highest and best. When you put me asunder, you sacrifice the sanctity of your own being. For Earth is sacred, and when you show disrespect for me, you disrespect your own life and its sacredness.

Know that I love you no matter what. I guard your life with my life, but I am dying. I cannot sustain this energy of man any longer. I am weary and I am tired. My substance has lost its colour, its energy, its nutrients, and its zest for living. I feel unloved and saddened.

Yet there is hope. There are many lightworkers on Earth, assisted by beings of light, who are assisting me with rising out of the Third Dimension to begin my new life as the spirit of the Fifth Dimension. I will be clean and pure again, and the life I will sustain will be green, bright, and brimming with love for all things sacred and pure. There will be such joy in living. The abundance I will bring will be respected by all those who have chosen to rise with me. There will be no exploitation, pollution, greed, or corruption. The life I will carry will be of my own heart, and I rejoice in this knowledge.

Bless the Earth as you walk upon me. Hold me in awe and reverence. Bring Creator's light down to my diamond core and help me replenish my energies. I must store up my resources, for the energy I expend at the time of ascension will be immense. I cannot tell you how joyous I feel at this coming in of the new age. It will bring great sacrifice for many, but the need is great. Let me tell you now that there is no wisdom in staying upon me after ascension, for I will be gone within a year. Come with me, my children, and let us herald in the new age of life, love, and light for the children of the future. The universe is ready, and so am I.

Are you?

AIR

Archangel Michael Speaks

Air is an element that is difficult for humans to grasp the concept of, for it is around you but cannot be seen. It is an unknown quantity as far as sacredness, for it blows ill in some parts due to pollution, pesticides, human waste, and smog. Air is of the winds. It is an essential part of the Earth's atmosphere, and it sustains all life. It is of essence, but it is invisible to the naked eye. It cannot harm when it is still, but it is a force to be reckoned with in a storm.

You feel air around you. You feel it moving, you breathe it in and you exhale it. It is of you and in you. You are one with it in more ways than you can know. Air is of the mountains, of the lakes, and of the highlands and lowlands. It is clear and it is polluted, but it still *is*.

The sacredness of air is in its connection to Mother Earth and to the *all*. Air gives life, which is sacred. Air nourishes the human body with oxygen and plant life with carbon dioxide. Life is a gift from God and allows all souls to learn their lessons and to spiritually evolve. The purer the air you breathe, the healthier your body will be. Your body is your temple. The more respect you show it, the longer you will live, and the better your quality of life will be.

Mother Earth began life in a pristine condition. All elements of air, fire, water, and earth were untouched and unpolluted by human hands. The plants and animals coexisted with the elements as was intended. The sacredness of life was matched by the purity of the elements. Thos days have gone, yet there is still hope. When Mother Earth has ascended, her heart will be whole again and her ability to sustain purity in her elements will be greatly enhanced. It is up to man to commit to the promise that ascension brings and to raise his vibrations in accordance with those of the Earth. When he has done so, the urge to maintain purity in all things will be greater and the quality of life as you know it will be greatly improved.

When you breathe polluted air, drink polluted water, grow things in malnourished soil, or use fire in a way that is harmful to your body, you show yourself disrespect. You desecrate the sacredness of your temple, which is holy and sacred because it is at one with the *all* and at one with Creator. Life is sacred, and all that sustains life is also sacred. Air sustains life and is at one with it. Breathe in only what sustains you. If you cannot avoid breathing in polluted air, show respect to your body by cleansing it with the purest water and the healthiest, purest food. Ask the Masters for assistance in cleansing the elements. We are always with you, but you must ask.

The air that you breathe carries God's particles. They are the particles of creation called adamantine particles. They come with the sunlight. They are in the breeze, carried on the wind, and caught in the rain. Adamantine particles are the gift of creation. When you breathe them in and consciously breathe them out as love and light, you create God's world. His world is one where all are united in a web of peace, love, and harmony.

Breathe in light and breathe out love. Every breath you take is the breath of God. He does not leave you breathless; only fear can block the breath of God. When you breathe as God does, you breathe pure love and creation. You create a web of love that encircles the world and creates a sense a sense of peace and oneness. Send your love on the wind. Breathe it out with intention and love. Feel it go out into the world. See it spread as light over the planet. Dwell in harmony and peace. Know love. Breathe love. You are love.

That is all there is.

I AM Archangel Michael.

Exchanging Energy

Mother Mary Speaks

The laws of giving and receiving, polarity, and abundance require energy to be exchanged in order for a balance to exist between the persons making the exchange.

Energy is in all things. In fact, everything in the universe is energy. Energy is expended in many ways, and as it is expended, it must be replaced. There is nothing that can function without its energy force being replenished, and this includes human energy.

If you expend energy on someone else and it is not replaced, then you will become drained and unbalanced. The energy exchange must be of equal value to the energy that was given. If not, there will still be a lack of balance, and illness or disequilibrium may occur.

Money is energy, but it does not have to be the gift of exchange. As long as the exchange is of equal value and is agreed on by both parties, there will be balance and harmony, and the gift that was given will take full force. Know that when you give of your energy freely, but it is not recognised or valued, your self-esteem is affected and your soul is left malnourished. Reflect on this the next time you feel that your gift has gone unnoticed, and allow yourself to receive in other ways that replenishes your energy and brings you back into balance. In other words, bring into focus the energy that has not been exchanged, and be open to receiving from the universe to replace the energy that has been expended.

Your body, mind and spirit will benefit greatly, and you will feel balanced, energised and in-tune with the world.

That is all.

TIME

Saint Germaine Speaks

Time does not exist. The universe does not operate on time. There are conditions on the use of time on the Earthly Plane, but no such conditions operate in the wider universe. Time can be manipulated and traversed, as long as it is for the higher good of all. The limitations man has put upon himself on Earth in relation to time are many, and they create blockages to the possibilities and opportunities that are open before you. When you do not live under the illusion of the barriers of time, there is a freedom that allows for greater channels of communication amongst species and between planes of existence. After ascension, the barriers of time will begin to come down, but it will take some time for man to adjust to the removal of the illusions of the Third Dimension.

Traversing the barriers of time will open up new possibilities for communication and travel. Think back to a time when you were late and you had a long distance yet to travel. You feared you would not make it in time, yet the other party was late also. Or think of a time when time dragged so slowly that you thought the day/night would never end. If man were to free himself from such restrictions and simply hold the intention of being in the time and place that he needed to be, while trusting that would be so, it would indeed be so!

The Fifth Dimension will begin to bring down the illusions man has carried about time and space. It will be possible to communicate with a thought, and it will not be necessary to carry a phone or a computer. Distance will now be a problem of the past. It is not that the Earth will operate without time. The organisation of your structures will also allow for a keeping of time to maintain order. Yet the restrictions around time will become less commonplace. Humans will be vibrating at much higher frequencies. They will be much more in tune with each other. Their connections to each other will be of a much higher order. When one is vibrating at the same frequency as another, the connection is strong. You call it being "in tune" with one another. The airwaves will be alive with thought patterns that communicate and reverberate around the world. In the new dimension, after ascension, time will not be a barrier as it once was, but many people will need to know how to traverse the timeline for the highest and best purposes. It can be used for your own advantage, as long as its use does not contravene anyone else's free will. When people know how to use time to their advantage and can traverse the timeline with ease, communications will move to telepathy and the world will be more united.

This is the way of the future.

And so it is.

About the Author

Victoria Cochrane, MEd (Hons), is a spiritual healer, psychic reader and medium who lives on the North West Coast of Tasmania with her husband Richard. They have three adult boys.

Victoria is a Reiki master and an Advanced Theta Healing (R) practitioner. Her work encompasses raising the vibrations of the Earth through sending healing to the planet every day. She also helps people work through their negative belief patterns and childhood and/or past life issues so they can begin their own spiritual journeys and discover their higher life purpose. She runs spiritual development courses to empower others to find their own spiritual and psychic gifts and produces a spiritual newsletter, which is blogged monthly.

Victoria has been channelling the Masters and the Creator for eight years. Since first publishing this book she has published two more. 'Beyond Ascension 2012: The Highest Truth' was first published in 2013 (Balboa Press) and has now been revised and re-published under her own banner, Victoria Cochrane Publications (Ingram Spark/Lightning Source). She recently re-released her third book, The Alignment of the Universe: Messages from Other Worlds (2016, Ingram Spark/Lightning Source).

www.victoriacochrane.com
www.reachingoutspiritualnews.blogspot.com.au

Lightning Source UK Ltd.
Milton Keynes UK
UKHW011844240722
406304UK00001B/42